From the desktop of Jeffrey Simmons

A vacation in Paris inspired Miroslav Sasek to create childrens travel guides to the big cities of the world. He brought me *This is Paris* in 1958 when I was publishing in London, and we soon followed up with *This is London*. Both books were enormously successful, and his simple vision grew to include more than a dozen books. Their amusing verse, coupled with bright and charming illustrations, made for a series unlike any other, and garnered Sasek (as we always called him) the international and popular acclaim he deserved.

I was thrilled to learn that *This is Paris* will once again find its rightful place on bookshelves. Sasek is no longer with us (and I have lost all contact with his family), but I am sure he would be delighted to know that a whole new generation of wide-eyed readers is being introduced to his whimsical, imaginative, and enchanting world.

Your name here

Published by arrangement with Simon & Schuster Books for Young Readers,
Simon & Schuster Children's Publishing Division

This edition first published in 2004 by
UNIVERSE PUBLISHING
A Division of Rizzoli International Publications, Inc.
300 Park Avenue South
New York, NY 10010

*See updated Paris facts at end of book

2004 2005 2006 2007 2008 / 10 9 8 7 6 5 4 3 2 1

Printed in the United States of America

ISBN: 0-7893-1063-5

Library of Congress Catalog Control Number: 2003114670

Cover design: centerpointdesign
Universe editor: Jane Ginsberg

M. Sasek

This
is
Paris

POSTES 20ᶠ REPUBLIQUE FRANÇAISE

UNIVERSE

So here we are.

There are ten million people living here
in the capital of France, one big river —
the Seine — dozens of monuments, dozens
of churches, dozens of museums — and
thousands of cats.

This one is called
Kiki

— and this is Joseph.

And here is Rita,

the grocer's cat. But of course cats aren't
the only things, there are people, too.

This lady is called a concierge.

She is a sort of guardian angel,

and there is one for many houses in Paris.

Here is a "dame" bringing home a long loaf — like a thick stick.

This man is drawing a picture of
Notre-Dame on the pavement.

This is the churchwarden of Notre-Dame

— the cathedral of Paris. It took two hundred years to build. The first stone was laid in 1163. Henry VI, King of England, was crowned here and so was Napoleon I of France. Inside the cock that stands on top of the weather-vane there is a holy relic — parts of the original crown of thorns.

And here is Notre-Dame itself.

Just a little way off from Notre-Dame we find
the Bird Market, which is held every Sunday.

This is called the Conciergerie.

During the French Revolution Queen Marie Antoinette, the revolutionary leaders Robespierre and Danton, and 2,300 other people were imprisoned here before they were executed. At one corner of the building is the Clock Tower, with the oldest public clock in Paris. It dates from 1330.

This is what a bus-stop is like.

And here comes the bus.

This is the way down to the Métro (underground or subway).

This is the platform.

— And here comes the train. It always has five coaches.
The red one in the middle is first-class.*

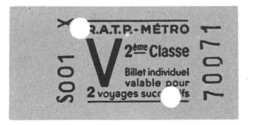

And here's your ticket.

This is the Holy Chapel,
Sainte-Chapelle, built for
King Louis (who became
Saint Louis) six hundred
years ago.

This is the Pont-Neuf.

It means "the new bridge," but actually it's the oldest one in the whole city.

This is the pleasure-boat you
take when you go for a trip
down the river Seine.

You find these bookstalls on the embankment of the Seine. You can buy old maps and pictures here as well as second-hand books.

This is the oldest church in Paris, St. Germain-des-Prés.

They started building it nearly a thousand years ago.

This is a "bistro," where you can
get anything you like to drink — and
perhaps something to eat as well.

This is called a "café-tabac,"
where they sell other things too —
chewing-gum and ball-point pens
and even postcards and stamps.
There's always a letter-box nearby.

Here is another sort of letter-box

— and still another, inside a lamp-post.

This is a fire-alarm

— and a call-box for ringing up the police.

Here is the Panthéon.

Many famous Frenchmen are buried here:
Rousseau, Voltaire, Victor Hugo and lots
of others.

This is the Jardin du Luxembourg.
Jardin means Garden. Here you can hire
your own toy sailing-boat.

This is the central market for all
Paris, called "les Halles."*

This is what the street-sellers
look like here.

Here is one of the porters in the
Halles. They call him "un fort"
— a strong man — because he
can carry half a carcass of beef
on his shoulder.

Here's another strong man.

You can see him weight-lifting on the main streets.

And you might see this fire-eater too.

This is the Opera, one of the biggest theaters in the world.

It is almost as high as the towers of Notre-Dame.

Here is a flower-girl.

This church is called the Madeleine,
and it looks like a Greek temple. In the beginning
Napoleon wanted to have it as a temple to the
glory of his soldiers.

This square is called the Place Vendôme.
The column was made by melting down 250 Russian and
Austrian cannons captured by Napoleon at the battle of
Austerlitz.

These are the Republican Guards.

Now we are looking at the most famous museum in the world, the Louvre.* If you go inside, you will see the Mona Lisa.

Here she is, as Leonardo da Vinci
painted her.

This arch is called the Arc de Triomphe du Carrousel. If you stand underneath it you can see the other arch over two miles away, the Arc de Triomphe de l'Etoile.

You can see some of these different kinds of lamp-posts in Paris.

This is the Place de la Concorde. King Louis XVI, his queen, Marie Antoinette, and hundreds of others were guillotined here during the Revolution. But the name means "Harmony Square." The Obelisk of Luxor that stands in the middle is over three thousand years old. It was brought here all the way from Egypt.

This is called the Rue du Chat qui Pêche, Street of the Fishing Cat. It is only two yards across.

And here is the Champs-Elysées, a mile-and-a-half long. It is lined with fine shops and cafés and cinemas.

At one end of it is a garden where you can ride on a donkey.

And at the other end is the Arc de Triomphe de l'Etoile — the one we saw before from the distance — which Napoleon had put up to celebrate his victories. In the middle of it is the Tomb of the Unknown Soldier.

This waiter's name is Marcel. When you want him you call "Garçon!" — Boy! — even though he's sixty years old.

Here is Monsieur Dupont, the policeman. He blows his whistle and twirls his stick to make the traffic go faster.

Here is another policeman on a bicycle. When they ride along like this, the Parisians call them "hirondelles" — swallows.* This one's name is also Monsieur Dupont.

Dupont is just as common a name in France as Smith in England or America.

This building is the Invalides, built by King Louis XIV
for disabled soldiers. Inside is the tomb of Napoleon.

Everyone knows the
Eiffel Tower

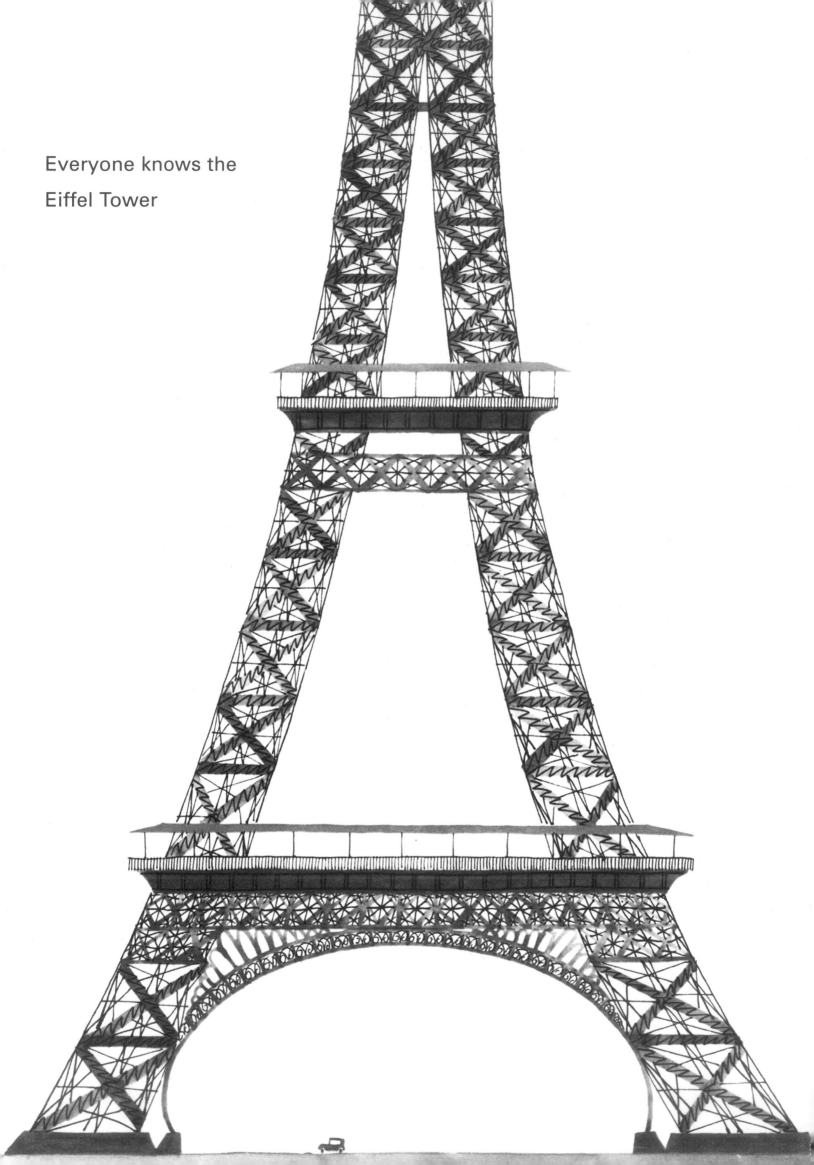

— which is one thousand and sixty-three feet high. When you are on the top you can see for about thirty miles in every direction. If you want to go up, you must climb 1,665 steps — unless you take the lift!

This is the statue of Joan of Arc.

And here is Joan of Arc herself in prison at the Grévin Museum. You can see many other famous people here too, ancient and modern — in wax.

These are the painters of
Montmartre painting the church of
the Sacré-Coeur, the Sacred Heart.

Here is the Sacré-Coeur itself. From the top
of the steps you have the most beautiful view
in the city.

This nun's name is Sister Mary. She belongs to the Order of St. Vincent de Paul.

But this woman is not a nun at all. She is a Breton peasant from the country-side on a visit to Paris.

This column stands in the Square of the Bastille. In the old days there was a prison here which the people of Paris took by storm at the beginning of the French Revolution.

Here is a butcher's where they sell only horse-meat.

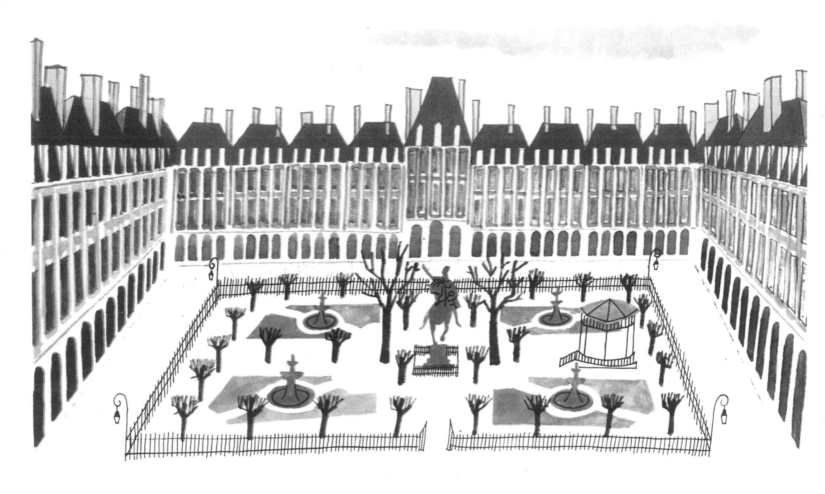

This square is called Place des Vosges. Victor
Hugo used to live at Number Six.

In the Jardin d'Acclimatation you can get a certificate for good driving from a real policeman.

And here is the little train to take you there from the Porte Maillot.

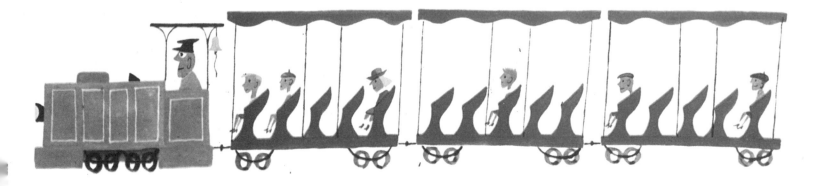

This is the Monkeys' Paradise in the zoo.

Here is the Flea Market, where you can buy anything from a trumpet or a periscope to an African spear.

Fifi is fresh from the coiffeur.

Ever since the year 1881 there has been a law
that you musn't stick posters on this wall.

Here is a Moroccan selling
his carpets.

This is a cemetery for dogs on the Clichy bridge.

And this is the

And now it's your turn to see Paris with your own